Reflections in the Mist

Collected Poems 2021-2022

by David A. Folds

WingSpan Press

Published in the United States and the United Kingdom
by WingSpan Press, Livermore, CA

The WingSpan name, logo and colophon are
the trademarks of WingSpan Publishing.

Publisher's Cataloging-in-Publication Data
Names: Folds, David A.
Title: Reflections in the mist : collected poems 2021-2022 / David A. Folds.
Description: Livermore, CA : Wingspan Press, 2023. | Summary: Poems on a
variety of subjects including social history, travel, music, death, nature, health,
awareness, and the psychedelic times of the 1960s.
Identifiers: LCCN: 2023900372 | ISBN 9781636830452 (pbk.) | ISBN
9781636839660 (ebook)
Subjects: LCSH: Elegiac poetry. | Nature – Poetry. | Poets, American – 21st
century. | United States – History – 20th century – Poetry. | BISAC: POETRY
/ General. | POETRY / American / General. | POETRY / Subjects & Themes /
General.
Classification: LCC PS3606.O43 R44 2023 | DDC 811 F--dc23
LC record available at https://lccn.loc.gov/2023900372

First edition 2023
Printed in the United States of America

www.wingspanpress.com

1 2 3 4 5 6 7 8 9 10

Reflections in the Mist

THIS IS DEDICATED

TO THOSE WHO GAVE ME

ENCOURAGEMENT AND DIRECTION

TO DEVELOP AND PRESENT THESE WRITINGS:

MY WIFE VICKIE

MY BROTHER CHUCK AND HIS WIFE JANE

(BOTH PASSED AWAY IN 2022)

AND ALAN BAXTER AND EVIE IVY

Back from the Philippines

we left our hotel

in Tacloban

very early

four am

off to the 3rd world

no frills airport

set for hours of waiting

our patience demanding

after a long eventually

we were called to board

a smallish jet

climbing the stair structure

for a short flight

David A. Folds

in Cebu back on land

we followed directions

to find our luggage

then hailed a cab

for a ride to our near

overnight hotel

the room was an upgrade

a suite with more

space than we

could ever use

gathering early morning

a hearty buffet-breakfast

and a quick front desk

check out

then back to the airport

    but this time

        international

what a difference

    was this 2-year-old one

modern design

    high arching ceilings

beautiful wood structuring

    throughout

no 3rd world

    lingering feeling

a modern process

    leading to a

non-stop flight

    half day

        confinement

David A. Folds

to finally land amid

the overwhelming

prosaic JFK

relieved exhausted

in some ways

happy

we connected to

our car-service

sat back awaiting

arrival soon

back in

Jersey City

1/9/2021   Jersey City, NJ, USA

Night Glow

the night slips in

    when you least

        expect it

stirring moods

    of memories

        long forgotten

briefly captured

    as someone

        you thought

        you were

but never knew

    or even cared for

David A. Folds

moments seem to

hang suspended

without a flow

of continuity

no lesson learned

then tossed away

we would look

for reason

while there is really

nothing there

a traffic-light

blinking yellow

not synchronized

to help the traffic

branches swaying

obedient leaves

must flutter

a rising moon

      full flushed

         in color

softly shouts

      its strength

         for silence

claims its birthright

      a time for calm

bathe in its rays

      and things seem

         briefly balanced

1/21/2021   Jersey City, NJ, USA

David A. Folds

Anarchy in Our Midst

amazing how many

Americans

miss the point

our land our culture

is supposed to reflect

an inclusiveness

ancestors came freely or not

but the philosophy

grew

towards universal freedom

tolerance for all

lawful beings

a central three part

structure

set to balance

national control

to seek to find

    a middle

        compromise

it's not just mine

    it's not just yours

a president

    who would brook no failure

        to his warped ideas

has led a muddle headed

    petulant mob

toward anarchistic

    unamerican

        insurrection

how strongly

    can the stupid

    gather

oh how much we still

    need to grow

1/9/2021   Jersey City, NJ, USA

David A. Folds

Music in Our Life

the wind rolls past

    the mundane moments

while I wonder

    where I am today

but listening to a song

    that reaches inside

past the defenses

    of inward restraint

the flow of tempo

    reaches out to grab

while the tune floats pitch

    in hopeful ascension

then lowering to soften

    the reality of our wishes

I'm carried along

    traveling on a

        sonic journey

all too short

    but truly blissful

left with a buzz

    and internal echoes

that filter in with

    the seconds of life

        staring me in the face

the prosaic non-music

    of these tone-deaf

        rhythmless times

misses the beauty

    of created cohesion

misses the fullness

    of complete involvement

while I look to fill

    in the blank

life continues

    inspired or not

1/13/2021   Jersey City, NJ, USA

David A. Folds

Weather

the rain surrounds

    the barren branches

      of weather

        stripped trees

no leaves to gather

    moisture

only their roots

    try to gather from a

      cold hard earth

seasonal hibernation

    descends upon us

pointed patterns of rain

    drip into muddied

      growing puddles

as we watch the downpour

from our protective

windows

not a time to venture out

to swim in the

turmoil of nature

sit back

read a book

peace to be found

in the quiet

of the moment

1/18/2021   Jersey City, NJ, USA

David A. Folds

A Journey of Perception

let us walk for awhile

in the kaleidoscope

of life

along the curvatures

of the shore

under grey-white clouds

looking across the water

a fog plays hide and seek

with images of

towers climbing

into the mist

the water flowing

out towards

the sea

a pleasure liner glides

    slowly past us

warning with its

    sea horn

we stroll by

    the other way

fade out in memory

return to the waters

    of the joy

        of my youth

canoeing in the

    confusion

        of my times

green surface to

    the lakebed's garden

        of slippery seaweed

David A. Folds

the colonies of floating

lily pads blanketing

near the shore

beauty of sadness

weeping willows

grasp the summer air

home to muskrats

before we came

even they avoid

the snapping turtles

the wind and occasional

motored boats push

ripples through

the quiet lake

on the hills of the

enveloping trees

hide the incidental homes

looking out at

the floating calm

in the city

   the chaos rules

      without a question

when I first came

   Fifth and Madison

      were still two-way

streets surviving

   somehow

imagine buses moving

   in and out in that

      compressed space

away from the park

   where was the grass

      all cement and no dirt

nothing moved in slow time

   except the snarled

      jammed-up traffic

David A. Folds

nothing built from God

and everything built

for money

everyone moving fast

to their righteous

urban destinies

in the arms of

blessed Barcelona

people move about

without the face of sadness

of the cold feel

of most cities

the buildings built to

breath with

character

Catalan spirit

embracing the culture of

yesterday and now

the last day found

one demented soul

plunked on the sidewalk

screaming from

inner pain

even there

among the beauty

it is possible

by the shore

in Torremolinos

looking out at

the vastness of

the Mediterranean

it was feeling more like

a vast lake

David A. Folds

it was a calm

hot shiny day

occasional tourists

like us

did not produce

the madness

of Manhattan

compared to it

little was here

but the pulse

of life smoothly

flowed at a

calming pace

nothing was

      insisting

only the timing

      of the tour bus

next day

      declared demands

soon our escape

      would be lost

we would be flying

      over big water

traveling

      back to our home

to find our local

      chance for peace

1/30/2021 Jersey City, NJ, USA

David A. Folds

Out to Sea

the vessel glides

out from the shore

ripples flowing

rhythmically

out from both sides

patterns on the surface

of ribbed

moving water

we move forward

floating in a

cushion of change

winds catch the angle

of our welcoming sail

now soft rocking

responds

to the casual waves

we relax with an

    edge still awaiting

half in control

    the reality of vastness

      intrudes

and we catch

    a lungful

      of salty air

in the early morning light

2/25/2021   Jersey City, NJ, USA

David A. Folds

Question Mark

does the cold

       bring the wind

does the sea

       bring the land

will the moments

       find a sparkle

as tomorrows fog

       restive minds

the adventure

       of perception

flies fully

       toward our darkness

visions float

       to lost horizons

cries doubling

       over laughter

time is wrestling

    with the stillness

as dripping clocks

    confuse the hour

we walk from shadows

    into light

to confiscate

    all confusion

but questions still

    arise again

blink once and they

    will not be gone

we will never

    find the answers

to perplexities

    of everything

3/5/2021   Jersey City, NJ, USA

David A. Folds

Curtain of Air

a fog sneaks in

  enveloping

    unsuspecting air

across to Manhattan

  past the assumed

    Hudson River

no outlines of buildings

  are seen through

    this curtain

      of moisture

you believe

  you know what's there

but your eyes say

  nothing's there at all

look for a few

    darker forms

pushing past

    the wall of off-white

until then

    rest and wait

        for beginnings

          of clearing

happy not to be

    lost in confusion

        out upon the water

3/25/2021 Jersey City, NJ, USA

David A. Folds

Lost Moments

soft songs whisper

remembrances

fading out of sight

music from distant

memories can never

reach your space

the flow of moments

rushes past

with not a chance

to savor

worlds spin and flow

breathe in expansion

then exhaling

as they shrink

the sight and sound

of experience

impacts and then echoes

far into later times

to think of what has

passed before

and cannot be

reached again

4/18/2021 Jersey City, NJ, USA

David A. Folds

In the Pandemic

the flow of moments

rushes past

with not a chance

to savor

after the rain baptizes

all the open ground

the first strains of rays

slowly climb the horizons

initially a yellow red

embarrassed by its

intrusive arrival

while natural beings awaken

to their photosynthesis

but we unnatural altered ones

choose our independent

schedule

as many small rituals

      need completion

before we can stroll

      out our opened door

he was surgically masked

      down the hallway

           and down the elevator

through the lobby

      out the front door

freshness lined with

      remaining humidity

surrounded his being

      flushed into his lungs

striding through

      the planned developed

          neighborhood

David A. Folds

along the side walk

crossing paths

with masked or unmasked

or half-masked

mysterious beings

he stepped to the side

or turned his head

away from any passing

offenders

he was vaccinated but still

uncertain

will this protect

completely

could he gain the

molecule

be well but

pass it to others

no one seemed

really sure

he reached his first

destination

the day to search

fortune buying lottery

tickets in pocket

on to the coffee shop

stand in line

six feet distanced

just for a coffee

just for his

egg sandwich

David A. Folds

returning back home

passing the masked

and those not observing

while the sun now showed

more brilliance

more fiery yellow

searing off the

humidity

reaching towards a normal

in this time that

lacks much of our

human normal

while time will not wait

but will laugh

at our frustration

4/29/2021   Jersey City, NJ, USA

My City Arises

the city is like myself

externally bombarded

from all sides

fleeting awareness

unremembered

unrecorded

internal energy

radiating

more outward

than in

the city embraces with

love or disgust

its massive

organic totality

heat baked cement

and steel

in Summer

create an irritated edge

even to breath

David A. Folds

cold structures in Winter

reach up towards

the warmth

not high enough

to negate

a chilled existence

rare accidental

structuring

allows an echo

of sounds

but the blaring blasts

of urban energy

seek out the quiet

places

dying like

old skin cells

trying to hang on

urban culture

feeds the creative

from the cacophony

     of stranded moments

to the quiet

     of hidden lives

we rejoice in

     our togetherness

          when it suits us

and focus on

     the differences

          from historic habit

somehow

     the city of myself

pauses in reflection

     sitting in wonderment

trying to figure out

     how we all got here

5/21/2021   Jersey City, NJ, USA

David A. Folds

Enigma

the flow of moments

  rushes past

    with not a chance

     to savor

the leaves flutter

  in the wind

     like frantic green wings

the beginning of time

  is still always

passing like

    a fading train

and we don't know

  so much that goes

    on around us

listen to the language

    of the birds

knowledge spread

    without our understanding

the breath of nature

    flows over

        our structured world

we wade through it

    caged in our ego-centric

      perception

trying to catch eternity

    with a butterfly net

5/12/2021   Jersey City, NJ, USA

　　　　　　　　　　　　　　David A. Folds

Echoes

but I have washed

my hands

of it

why do thoughts

return ... hinting

an unbreakable

union

gone, I know

but doggedly

reappearing

the words struck

through

teeth deep into

the moment's

psyche

it was briefly

all encompassing

full reality

wellness was

overcome

peace was

destroyed

I knew my being

was not an

impenetrable

brick wall

balance undone

as from a seismic

disruption

whose echoes own

reappearance

floating in

to thoughts

not wanted

we are still the masters

of our own

imprisonment

5/24/2021   Jersey City, NJ, USA

David A. Folds

Stagnation

he was not the darling

of the amused

self-praising

crowd

the wallflower

quietly presuming

nothing at all

still ... half afraid

of motion to draw in

staring questions

in a corner of

self-imposed silent

outcasts

insecure

out of place

lost in the

    uselessness

        of floating time

the resounding chaos

    of layers

        of communal

            chatter

encompass

    the flattened bed

        of consciousness

no spark to stroke

    the pleasure centers

had thought he should

    present himself

social propriety

    required attendance

David A. Folds

in the corner

wondering if

anything mattered

frozen psyche

lost in inertia

why not just leave

well, maybe,

a little later

5/25/2021   Jersey City, NJ, USA

Innovators

they come to us

out of the

cosmic rainbow

like a quickly

passing

torrent of rain

the prophets

of truths

discoveries

and spirit

one in a million

or more likely

one in a

billion

upsetting some

or sometimes

every beloved

convention

David A. Folds

stirring up

    the curious

        briefly

causing a historic

    ripple effect

sometimes

    accumulating

tidal waves

    towards a

        life changing

          tsunami

creating milestones

    of history

like each DNA

    alteration

that reformed

    our ancient

        predecessors

towards

    today's humanity

prophets

    are attacked

slaughtered

    for their

        audacity

we praise those

    of the past

who suffered

    within their

        own timetable

to leave a legacy

    for the growth

    of us all

deserving

    or not

7/7/2021   Jersey City, NJ, USA

47   David A. Folds

Moon Phase

the moon painted patterns

over the rippling

peaceful waters

ignoring the intensity

of early evening

energy

people tired but not

yet slowed down

while Planet Earth built

with internal

combustion

contains all phases

of peace and war

and we walking

upright two-legged

also own these

two extremes

we possess more

power than

we experience

not what we

draw in from

the outside

nor what we express

outwardly

from within

but what hides inside

and resonates within

if we learn

to open the passage

meanwhile the moon

slides south

above us

waiting for our

moment

to find its peace

6/19/2021   Jersey City, NJ, USA

49   David A. Folds

Organic Growth

like blossoming flowers

I curl up and rest

in the cooling

night glow

and half-hibernate within

the winter's chill

my roots seek

their succulent

nutrient needs

and the Sun's heat

feeds my

growing energy

I expand my space

like a climbing vine

accumulating a little more

of the vast stretch

of space and time

Spring explodes with

starts and stops

stretching the arms

of plants to meet

the warmth

Summer radiates

through the excesses

of our growth

while Autumn slows our

steps within the colors

of dropping leaves

and Winter draws us

into the contemplation

of our inner being

trying to search

to relocate

life's balance

6/22/2021   Jersey City, NJ, USA

David A. Folds

1802 Chicago Avenue

the rhyme of this address

has easily remained

in my memory

for 75 years

that long ago

there was a large

oldish house

seated as residence

on the corner of

Chicago and Clark Street

one block from the

main campus

of the eminent

Northwestern U.

we moved from

New Hampshire

in '46

I was 5 and a half

in the Summer

scheduled to attend kindergarten

in a new environment

that fall

I still remember the smell

and coloring

of lilac bushes

starting my

Evanston education

I would walk south

towards a kindergarten

through 6th grade

grammar school

everything was

respectable

everything was

safe

David A. Folds

from '34 until '72

Evanston

was dry

liquor to be had

on Howard Street

from the border

with Chicago

the house was too large

for us alone

we would rent out

a room to a

graduate student

and still controlled

more space than

we needed

great for an

overactive child

upstairs had

four bedrooms

a basement an attic

    and a large porch

gave many places

    to play or hide

there was a large

    staircase

        with an old-style

          banister

a two-door entry

    with a vestibule

the inner door's

    upper half had glass

in excitement with a parade

    to pass by our house

I ran back and forth

    stopping myself

        with my right arm

through the door's glass

    breaking the pane

        with my pain

David A. Folds

my dad took me up

to the bathtub

to bleed there

while he picked

bits of glass

from my skin

before taking me

to hospital for stitches

I missed that parade

under the elevated porch

there was space

closed off by

slates of wood

things like lawn care

were stored there

sometimes I would get

inside looking

through the slats

at the passersby to and from

the college

to me half the world

became that house

the rest was external

in the adventures

of school

and neighborhood

peace was needed

by my mother

but chaos was

an intruder

in childhood

experience

learning the world

in a protected bubble

7/2/2021   Jersey City, NJ, USA

David A. Folds

Buildings

a building exists as an

artificial world

a satellite within

the spinning

satellite that arcs

visibly distant to

the solar form

that owns an eternal

internal explosion

we small beings

live in small

worlds

like these

the Sun trusts its

intergalactic

placement

the Earth trusts

the Sun to continue

to be

life forms must trust

the protection from

Mother Earth

and humans trust

the safety of

a building's world

if the Sun starts

to die

if the Earth loses

its planetary position

if a building caught

in neglect

collapses without

a care

worlds tumble

lost in the rubble

life erased

snuffed out

like a still smoking candle

7/5/2021   Jersey City, NJ, USA

David A. Folds

Bali and Some More

having side trips

with every visit

to the Philippines

in '97 we chose

Indonesia that time

starting in Jakarta

a huge traffic burdened

city of Islam

besides a paid

group tour

traveling around

was not easy

our hotel included breakfast

giving us coupons

for McDonald's

McDonald's had their

beef sandwiches

but no breakfast

a few days in

     Yogyakarta

        proved special

Borobudur Temple

     seeing the dawn

a World Heritage

     gem of uniqueness

        will always resonate

but in Bali

     the totality

        was unmatched

all our prepaid

     flights and hotels

        had been at about

          2,000 Rupiah

        to the US dollar

David A. Folds

the day we arrived in Bali

the South East Asian

economic crisis hit

every day the Rupiah

number rose

by our departure

the rate was

over 16,000

every out of pocket

payment was

beyond cheap

each day we rented

a car and driver

for $25 US

he functioned as

a driver guide

happy for

the business

everywhere we went

was a beautiful

photograph

the ancient Hindu temples

seemed to vibrate

with their specialness

rice terraces

old coastal structures

temples sitting

in a lake

their temple roofs

cascading upwards

each roof smaller

as they rose

some had as many

as ten roofs

David A. Folds

in Ubud we saw

a Hindu cremation

ceremony

so expensive

some need to wait years

time to gather

enough Rupiah

the beaches were peaceful

but like others

around the world

We would see a

mother daughter duo

topless on the sand

but not in

our hotel

every tourist favorite site

has some issues

but in Bali

the impact of

beauty and

uniqueness

override

any difficulties

someday

we want

to go again

7/10/2021 Jersey City, NJ, USA

David A. Folds

Raga and Tala

the floating alto

of an Indian flute

steps into

space and time

the veena adding

thoughtfully sad

sounds of spirit

an Ali Akbar Khan begins

a beautifully thoughtful

ascending line

forward with the

sharply piercing

metal strings

of his sarod

or a Shrivkumar Sharma

taps the rising tones

on his dulcimer like

santoor

we are flowing into a

      procession

            of tonal rapture

slowly repeated again

      and climbing

sound purifying

      the moments

            into peace

spirit lifting

      as notes rise

         in raga

            climbing flow

resettling as

      descending tones

         trip down

only to restate

      the uplifting

         theme

David A. Folds

the tapped soft

piercing rhythm

of the tabla

announces a new phase

intensity

up a step

a rhythm tala walks into

a woven complex

stepping structure

the foundation for

movement and

a spiritual journey

we have been absorbed

into a magic world

of tone and

tranquility

let the sound

swim into your

deepest being

7/18/2021   Jersey City, NJ, USA

Tripping

light the candle

    perfect paraffin

        and trip on

            into the night

the wax softly melting

    inter mixing tones

        sliding reshaping

a wave of recognition

    slips slowly

        into focus

and then

    floats by

        image fading

          out of mind

David A. Folds

searching for questions

while answers hide

their mystery

walls pulsate

breathing slowly

structure alive

losing its rigidity

the sharply defined

angles of our lives

bend and sway

perception explodes

without its filters

our eyes' doubled vision

lose its melded

compromise

sound seems to spread

into a new

dimension

and everything can burst past

the usual barriers

beautiful flowers

unwanted weeds

we can trek through

every experience

just seated there

down on our floor

until dawn slowly

slides in

awakening the quiet

of a return

to a tired normal

7/31/2021 Jersey City, NJ, USA

David A. Folds

Drifting

sing to me

    sweet mercy

I am far from

    being found

time revolves

    spun by Earth's

        rotations and

            arcing path

each turning moment

    to push experience

    forward

        unforgiving

I feel no spin

    no arcing trajectory

but locked in seconds

    turned to hours

days slip by

      to weeks and months

until another year

      looks back in wonder

I am asleep

      in a current

         in the river of life

         stepping slowly

           forwards or back

where is my target

      lost in stories

         of mounds of history

8/11/2021   Jersey City, NJ, USA

David A. Folds

Refocus

into the lost world

of hidden thoughts

my hopes hover breathlessly

waiting for a cascade

of passing moments

the time of now

laughs and scorns

as it transgresses

each instance's

favorite passing

the whirling interchange

of cocktail gossip

travels off

to nowhere

to fall off the edge

of a flattened

static Earth

images slowly evolve

into a false clarity

sounds haphazardly

invade with

no remorse

ideas from floating thoughts

swim in a river

of seduction

drawing me into a direction

without any profit

I wait without confidence

for a chance to dance

in the stream

of focused action

to flow in rhythm

to a life in love

with every moment's

purpose

9/11/2021   Jersey City, NJ, USA

David A. Folds

9/11 Again

now 20 years have

exactly fallen

since the collapse

of the towers

that disassembled

into massive coffins

three thousand died then

over 2 more thousand died later

from ingested

breathed in

poison

whose danger was belittled

by valued authority

cancer found a new ally and

more will still die early

because of that neglect

we watched the flames

the smoke

the massive collapse

the monstrous dust

floating above

destroyed structure

hiding the limbs of

lost hopes of blown out

chances of moments of love

those who try to learn anything

from this history

are still stunned by

the insanely stupid

thoughts that drew

satanic logic

into targeting

three thousand innocents

into a grave

of rubble

we hope we never forget

lessons learned

of the hell that visited us

twenty years ago

9/11/2021   Jersey City, NJ, USA

David A. Folds

The Flower of Bruges

as the morning

early light emerges

the petals of the flower

that is Bruges

gradually open

and display the beauty

of this UNESCO

world heritage site

hard to find so many remaining

medieval structures elsewhere

so loaded with character

each still living

with its own uniqueness

first viewing the gradually

changing main street angles

sidewalks between cobblestone streets

with their beautiful

well-aged buildings

leading to a town center plaza

Markt

beautiful on all four sides

with a thirteenth century belfry where

a flight of bell sounds

flow each hour from

it's high carillon

the major throughways

displaying occasional

horse carriages

pulled by large healthy hoofs

clapping on aged

cobble stones

sharp striking

shouting tones

David A. Folds

some steps away

from the plaza

winding through medieval glory

is the peaceful canal

graced with architecture

first born five to seven

centuries ago

boating on it

bringing both

energy and calm

passing centuries of stone

sculpted structures

the feelings are both

distant and close

brought from some earlier

incarnation

9/26/2021   Jersey City, NJ, USA

Moments

I speak to the wind

    as thoughts float away

knowledge is a game

    of past fury and

        present confusion

heat rips through the air

    of August

sunlight envelopes

    everything

sweat stained shirts

    measure the Fahrenheit

a subway station

    like a baking oven

David A. Folds

pavement reflecting

unseen rays

asphalt melting

slightly

the wind reshuffles

moments of heat

I speak to my psyche

as it drifts away

just meandering

it does not listen

it does not care

wish the world could

find compassion

watch the clock

devour Dali

laughter likes the

      echoes of sadness

blindness sees

      the fall of Spring

and deaf is the descent

      to winter

autumn slows

      the breath

         of Nature

we float on through it

      lost in smallness

        losing still

          another minute

4/5/2022   Jersey City, NJ, USA

David A. Folds

Seasons Change

dramatic Autumn enters

with rust red waving,

fluttering, and falling

webbed hand-like leaves

one tree half-bare

has been a concert hall

during fuller times

an unknown number of

avian vocalists at 5pm

gathered hidden

among the foliage

the sound would spread

the imagination

how many were

singing away

wind leads a dance

    of moving branches

        and remaining rust red

        appendices

the gusts find entry

    where my coat

        lacks full insulation

          chilling skin and bones

there is no more time

    for basking in the sun

the air is fresh

    but aggressively

        thrown at me

moments never wait for yesterday

11/3/2021   Jersey City, NJ, USA

David A. Folds

A Story of Health

for the young

      even for the not so young

            wellness is mostly assumed

occasional sickness

      only a brief moment

the hard reality of mortality

      is a vague shadow

while cuts mend and

      broken bones repair

our body is growing

      or at least sustaining

we stride with strength

      we move with

            measured quickness

we look to tomorrow

      to climb still further

            toward our experiential growth

life is seemingly eternal

      in our microcosmic perception

but there further

    in the continuing rooms of life

        different perceptions pervade

sustaining becomes

    the constant challenge

broken bones are slow to heal

    and may never be the same

illness becomes a danger to linger

    combining with other maladies

we learn that the physical time clock

    is constantly continuing

        and is not eternal

life's box of chocolates

    may have some surprises

        still awaiting

11/10/2021 Jersey City, NJ, USA

David A. Folds

Gulls

the seagull is a nasty bird

large

beautiful in flight

some with black-tinged

flowing white wings

like two graceful blankets

flapping streaming

high or low

their shrill squawks

drive through air

like darting arrows

they search for whatever

they can grab

or steal

there is no morality

    no manners

        Machiavellian

           to the extreme

bullying smaller birds

    feuding with other gulls

but still gliding

    and soaring high

        with a grace that

           we can envy

12/07/2021   Jersey City, NJ, USA

89   David A. Folds

Visions

the birth of Venus

    painted rising from the sea

idealize and fully formed

    modest in her nudity

      standing on a shell

as calm and peaceful

    as any birthed infant is not

blown to the shore

    by the winds of Zephr

and soon to be clothed

    in a large flowing cloak

this exquisite Botticelli depiction

declaring the visual standard

of Florentine females

so rarely achieved

then or now

was a blessing

to the world of art

but an unattainable image

for most ladies

who carry their beauty

in their own ways

inside and out

in face and form

and feeling

true ideals are inspiring

but realities are alive

as all women walk

in their own

birthed realities

12/24/2021   Jersey City, NJ, USA

David A. Folds

Cold

long into the last of night

the chill cold air

wove up and down

running and searching through

open and hidden spaces

heavier thicker flakes

dropped down

with more assurance

than their lighter

snowy cousins

that would float from high

in a meandering wavy dance

down the fierce currents of air

quickly these

    small bleached bullies

        sought the earth

            sought to gather

to clothe its surface

    with frigid blankets

        of gleaming whiteness

a magic transformation

to sleep protected with

    hoped for heat

        we wore more

lay under more

    thicker bedding

our heads covered

    dreaming of icicles shovels

        and slippery pavement

long into the last of night

1/30/2022 Jersey City, NJ, USA

David A. Folds

Thoughts

remembering the times

       you can not touch

while the rhythm of raindrops

       tap on a windowsill

sitting alone

       looking away from the sound

thoughts swim

       in liquid memory

searching for today's reality

       but lost in earlier moments

when peace and balance

       might have sustained

but why did he say that

       throwing chaos into the mix

as you absorbed

       a deep thrust assault

still left inside

       echoing on a long dark

       corridor of thought

try to find memory moments

    of beauty and acclaim

like the negatives

    not really there

        but bathed in positive

like the charm of Florence

    the vibrations

        of treasured Bach

the awesome panorama

    of Swiss mountains

a kaleidoscope

    of shapes and colors

        as our Sun sets

this rain should

    wash clean our thoughts

        not dampen our deeper moods

2/18/2022   Jersey City, NJ, USA

David A. Folds

Jane

through the hush

    of sweet sorrow

silence seeks a recompense

    for credit for kindness

for remembrances

    of moments

a smile that glowed

    a laughter that gathered

with the art of her

    special creations

a being both known

    and unknown

we experienced connection

    without complete understanding

the Earth will continue to spin

    arcing in its elliptical journey

the oxygen still

    offers its usage

      but not for her

not for those past

    the point of breath

we will sustain the nourishment

    for our lungs

and mourn the loss of

    a quiet warrior to life

still breathing

    in our remembrances

3/9-21/2022   Jersey City, NJ, USA

David A. Folds

Growth

it begins with the seed

    the promise of a future

the chance of

    a new fulfillment

seeds sprout roots and stalks

    and stalks burst arms

and arms grow

    leaves and buds

so that buds reveal flowering

    that transitions to

    another cycle

while the seeds of animals

    transform through a series

    of progressive

    metamorphoses

first formed

    a head shape

    attached to beginnings

    of a body torso

limbs futures appear

first like rounded buds

partitions within the head

start developing

separate areas

for the brain

eyes and ears begin to form

and bones from targeted tissue

a heart continues to grow

beating an insistent

rhythm of living

life's blood is already flowing

within the womb

or inside a hard egg shell

the pain and joy

has hardly begun

5/11/2022 Jersey City, NJ, USA

David A. Folds

Chuck

the heart can rule the mind

emotions can sweep across

the corridors of thought

when special pressure points

of awareness

overcome all other focus

the death of a brother

stuns my being

all my 81 years

he was part of my structure

the older sibling

after childhood

a parallel friend

equal in maturity

or the lack of it

Covid had a hand

    in his destruction

not the disease

    but the restrictions

with no gathering

    no jazz piano

eating was of cheaper food

    with no income

making for less health

    less strength

        less resistance

            more vulnerable

first loss of weight

    never had been so thin

a tear in his lung

    wrecked his breathing

intense pneumonia followed

    he never really recovered

locked in a never ending

    rehab world

        lacking any real progress

David A. Folds

during all this distress

        his wife Jane died

his heart dropped down

        another level

almost his entire existence

        had been about performing

        not possible after his illnesses

he saw no possible future

        no chance for recovery

the basic drive for life

        fought with a feeling of despair

        every day

the world has lost a fine jazz artist

and I have lost my brother

6/1/2022   Jersey City, NJ, USA

A Span of History

we came into 1900

on a wave of naive realism

tempered by

a forced practicality

saw the 1912 presidency

lip flop parties of politics

liberal Republicans of Lincoln

becoming the business based

conservatives

the Democrats teetered between

liberal and southern

self-contained comfort

then the war to end all wars

led into a roar

emanating in the 20's

moments of escape within

the confines of society

David A. Folds

until the excess exploded

depressing people globally

the sad stories of poor

squeezed by the whims

of too much greed

darkened the years

after the crash

trying to uplift

trenches of sadness

movies let us dream

swing let us dance

beyond the night

then the 40's proved that conflict

was far from over

dominating

our focus of fear

once again war dead

and wounded rose in status

like football stars

victory and defeat by sacrifice

followed by late 40's dressed in recovery

normalization and

the advent of the television

carrying a dread of being red

McCarthy lies and

Dulles's domino theory

we should all be within

the form, the mold

of perfect citizen

even though racism still lived

in many forms and spaces

one eye trained on the chance

of termination

advent of the ultimate bomb

but rhythm and blues and

country cocreated

earth vibrating rock

and we rolled into it

or tried to stay away

David A. Folds

freedom

    now

        forced itself

            towards the front

people determined

    to challenge

        at any cost

a war within society

electric rock evolved

    into hippy high journeys

        of open sexuality

without a pause

    without a thought of guilt

tempered by the dark cloud

    of the draft

by a seemingly never ending

    horror in Vietnam

until the war of a generation

    mercifully stopped

so that technology became

    the mother of transitions

electronic chips and

    motherboards advanced

    new and newer

their generations leaped

    forward every year

personal computers

    giant databases

    amazing smartphones

drew us into the internal

    world of media

    and gaming

away from our inner peace

everything is available

    at an instanced touch

everything but the forgotten

    cold moments of reality

7/6/2022 Jersey City, NJ, USA

David A. Folds

Wishes

the soft whisper

of tomorrow's chances

haunts the mundane landscape

of our present days

thoughts of what our egos

believe should develop

may never occur

fate lacks a consistent

flow of positive growth

and discovery

routine places dominoes

one after the other

day after day

in a straight or

detoured path

onward to the next day

where all will still

be much the same

we are locked into what

        we call our choices

only the imaginative

        the creative impulse

can carry us beyond

        with brief moments

        to discover

7/30/2022   Jersey City, NJ, USA

David A. Folds

Day's End

the moon half-hidden

among a bed of clouds

watched and waited

the breeze bringing soon

tomorrow

sought out all

the tired players

life slipping by

almost unrewarded

plants just bathed in sunlight

now wishing rain-soaked roots

people saturated

with the day's nonsense

look towards

a hiatus of variations

without the shadow of

earlier complications

we have breathed to survive

      breathed to seek success

but success of what and why

now breath to slow the pace

      slow the metabolism

not demanding action

      not ruled by stress

find a quiet place

      in your haven

find a peaceful place

      in your heart

9/3/2022   Jersey City, NJ, USA

David A. Folds

Newport Geese

the Canadian geese

    are mostly gone

apparently moved elsewhere

    without harm

      by building management

protected species

    migratory birds

      choosing to remain

seduced by

    local food provided

they became an

    every day attraction

parents waddling

    with their brood

I saw as many as

    sixteen together

handsome birds walking on

        sidewalks and streets

feeling safe

        from cars and people

but leaving their droppings

        everywhere

parents by 3 or 4

        with a gestation time

        of 28 days

a few years was enough

        to explode their numbers

pavements were painted

        with their contributions

while dog walkers dutifully

        picked up

        what pooch provided

David A. Folds

hundreds perhaps thousands of years

of migration instinct and practice

ruined by humans

trying to be kind

wild plants and animals

live with

the grace of Nature

let Nature provide or withhold

her bounty

10/5/2022 *Jersey City, NJ, USA*

Ravages of December

when the winter's wind

    chases the warmth away

blood rushes everywhere

    to heal the defeated balance

a failed attempted action

    but for the assistance of our clothes

a season's thickened coat

    a patterned flannel shirt

gloves and hat and hood

    to protect a body under siege

to retain internal temperature

    while our faces buffet the bitter cold

only partially protected

    with a woolen scarlet scarf

12/22/2022 Jersey City, NJ, USA

David A. Folds

Index of Poems by Titles

David A. Folds